Hypocrisy has a Face
and Other Writings

Hypocrisy has a Face
and Other Writings

Dina Kafiris

KU PRESS

Text copyright © Dina Kafiris.

The moral rights of the author have been asserted.

First published in 2024 by Kingston University Press

All rights reserved. No part of this publication may be reproduced or transmitted, in any form or by any means electronic or mechanical, including photocopy, recording, or any information storage and retrieval system, without prior permission of the publisher.

Every effort has been made to fulfil requirements with regard to reproducing copyright material. The publisher will be glad to rectify any omissions at the earliest opportunity.

A catalogue of this book is available from the British Library

ISBN 978-1-909362-77-2

Typeset in Aviano Royale, Garamond Premier Pro, Rafaella and Rufina.

Author image © Gianni Gardelli.

Editorial and Design by Kingston School of Art MA Publishing students, Chaya Chudasama, Imogen Crockford, Yasmien Ibrahim and Saumya Malik.

KINGSTON UNIVERSITY PRESS
Kingston University
Penrhyn Road
Kingston-upon-Thames
KT1 2EE

For my father

Previous Works

Versions of some poems have previously appeared in:

'War'/ 'Alitheia'/ 'Maria'/ 'Interrogating the Gunman': Wild Court, 2023
'In Giving': To Koskino, Australia, 2023
'Hypocrisy has a Face': The Glass, Issue Number 32, Spring 2020
'The Column': One Surviving Poem Anthology, In Case of Emergency Press, Australia, 2019
'Tree of Misfortune': Universal Oneness: An Anthology of Magnum Opus Poems from around the World, Authorspress, India, 2019
'The Blinding Light Circling Elpida, in one act': Original Plus, 2014
'Playing God': American, British and Canadian Studies, Special Issue: Creative Writing: New Signals, New Territories, Romania, Volume 20, 2013
'War'/ 'You Left Leaving'/ 'Hypocrisy has a Face'/ 'Nostalgia'/ 'Identity': The Glasgow Review, May edition 2010
'Friends, Indeed!'/ 'In his Memory': The Recusant, 2009
'The Mistress': Horizon Review, Issue 1/2008

Contents

Author's Note	xi
PART 1	1
Maria	3
The Mistress	4
Nostalgia	6
Hypocrisy has a Face	7
You Left Leaving	8
Identity	9
Another Day	10
Meeting of the Holy Synod	11
Rebirth	12
In His Memory	13
Playing God	14
War	17
Love	18
Faith	19
Friends, Indeed!	20
In Giving	21
The Blinding Light Circling Elpida, in one act	22
The Column	25
Tree of Misfortune	27
Interrogating the Gunman	29
Alitheia	31
PART 2	33
The Demon and the Hero	37
I	37
II	40
III	51
IV	54
Biography	57
About KU Press	59

Author's Note

Athens is a city adorned with remnants of a tumultuous past. I cannot emphasise this fact enough, particularly when it comes to addressing the issue of identity. It is the past that has preoccupied Greek poetry for many centuries. It only seems logical that, if we are to understand the Greek nation in its contemporary form, we need to acknowledge the influence history has had on what the city has become today.

It was early on in my apprenticeship years that I discovered that the core of a person's existence is determined by the ability to evaluate their relationship with their city. For this reason, when the time came to write about the Athenian capital, it was crucial that I first identify my own position towards my ancestral homeland. I realised that, in the quest to discover its boundaries, it was inevitable that one would have to question one's own limitations. Moreover, one cannot help but see one's reflection in its image.

In the first decade of the 21st century, the period in which most of these poems were written, Greece saw several changes of government, an escalating financial crisis, the rise of the far right, and a mass-media explosion that resulted in the foreign press presenting the Greek people in a lesser light than that deserved.

It was indeed a sad moment to witness a nation being subjected to harsh criticism and condemnation by their European neighbours – a historical re-occurrence that now seems unavoidable. It was a time when the political and social events that were to shape Greece's history became pivotal to the writers and intellectuals who fought to challenge injustices they no longer wished to ignore. If social change required us to act, then, in this instance, knowledge was the predominant factor that would ensure progress.

Literature is where the public turns when governments are unwilling to provide the truth. In Greece, this sentiment rang louder than the church bell of Saint Nikolaos Ragavas during the 1944 liberation of Athens from the German occupation. Writing is a political act. When governments speak loud, poets must speak louder. This notion of duty can only be described as an instinctive reaction to speaking the truth where it does not exist – a responsibility that has frequently fallen on the shoulders of well-respected writers. It is, without doubt, a role that has required one to approach it with caution. After all, few have the capacity to withstand the consequences that follow as a result.

The selected poems in this collection are, therefore, a last defence against hostility. What is an urban portrayal has subsequently turned into a homage to a beloved city. Athens has been presented as what I had understood the Greek capital to be – a metropolis that is undeniably human. What follows are poems that attempt to do justice to the image of a city so greatly misunderstood. The prose poem 'The Mistress' creates a fictitious account of the private lives of public figures, illustrating the dangers of misinformation and disinformation, as well as unaccountability. In 'Nostalgia', we see that the political and social landscape of Exarchia introduces much needed questions, after the future of the Athenian has been plunged into uncertainty. The modern-day love poem, 'You Left Leaving', concludes with an attack from members of the far right on an economic migrant, at a time when the country is facing a surge in illegal immigration. In the poem 'Another Day', a home invasion is about to disrupt the daily routine of an urban professional, as crime increases in the capital. 'Meeting of the Holy Synod' observes discontented youths trying to come to terms with the loss of their spiritual leader, when four days of national mourning for the Archbishop Christodoulos are announced. Last but not least, 'Tree of Misfortune' takes us from a London hospital to a couple's longing for their ancestral homeland of Greece, now amid the economic crisis.

In the post-truth era, literature – as a manifesto of logic and reason – is a necessity. Literature should not stray far from the front bench of the political game. It is here that poetry will find its rightful place. The epicentre of Greek thought, Athens, has managed to revive cultural politics in a time of crisis. Athens is a resilient city, and one whose immortality rests in the hands of its contemporary writers who, as public intellectuals, have come to praise both the ancient and modern city for their very existence. This collection is a testament to this understanding.

Dina Kafiris
June 2017

PART 1

Maria

Dear old man,

why do you sit alone
reflecting on a war fought long ago

on the young girl
who spent with you those last few days
leaving you with the promise of a kiss
on your return.

Did you not find solace
in the woman who later bore your children
as you scratch your head in grief...

With a sigh,
you place your newspaper on that park bench
to meet the gaze of passing lovers in an embrace.

Sitting opposite you,
I watch that tear slip away.
Here in this night full of stories,
you whisper her name,

Μαρία.

Kifissia, Athens, 15 September 2001

THE *M*ISTRESS

She,

Grand hostess of tongue-twisted lies, found comfort in this Art Deco gem – a small café dripping with intimacy, chattering lips, momentary pauses from working actors, writers of the exquisite and bohemian kind who congregated within its closed doors.

A historian, as she was known amongst the staff, singlehandedly turned this haunt into a butcher's kitchen. Because of her, the beloved Mr P, favoured as the next Nobel Laureate, stopped writing; a minister, name not mentioned, left her husband for his private secretary to spite him; Mr M, opening night, on his way to the theatre, caught his wife canoodling in the corner of the same café, with his own brother, rumoured to have fled to a monastery far from the glory of the stage.

'I'm no different from a social columnist,' she once exclaimed.
'I report the facts. A noble service for my fellow man.'

Ear to the wall, who would dare repeat her discoveries without permission.

She screened faces belonging to the withered and the unspoilt as they entered her slaughterhouse, thrust away from the winter's glare. Become she did, a witness to the mention of a name, sound of a kiss, explosions of laughter, whispers in corners hidden from the human stare (so they thought). She knew very well there existed secrets in every peck, each exchanged word, each message left on a mobile phone. Whilst Piaf's 'Les Amants de Teruel' played, lost behind the babble of voices, her leering look cautioned them.

But as scenarios continued to unravel, the cigarette hanging from her painted lips loosened, dry from the cold she so despised, exhaling smoke over the copy of *Henry and June*, given by him.

She stretched out a plump leg, having noticed a ladder in her stocking where her lover's fingers had travelled the night before. Through fake auburn curls, she caught the lingering eye of the man beside her. With no smile to offer, she concentrated on finishing her third coffee, slowly, ever so slowly, interrupted by thoughts of him.

The man who had promised her wildflowers from the Grampians, mud baths in Turkey, to sail the rivers of Myanmar…

Who would have imagined, Madeleine de la Rosa a mistress.

Athens, 28 October 2001

Nostalgia

In walks uncertainty. The disorientated anarchist. Her sculptured crown swamped with dreadlocks. Asks for directions. A harem of eyes studies her. She amuses some. No glances are met. They return to their conversations. Gaze at the entrance to the café. More absent expressions flock inside. Away from the season's bitter hold. Inside they seek the warmth. Reminiscing the lost summer. The smell of heat. Sun against their faces. It paints their frozen lips. Outside fumes smother the city. Cars crawl around the square. Motorbikes mount the pavements. Drivers throw their anger to the one in front. Pedestrians await the traffic lights. Stern faces. Pale. Pierced. Tattooed. Couples grasp each other. They kiss. The cold creeps by. Naked trees pose as the city bathes in its dread. One fears the days to come.

Athens, 12 July 2002

Hypocrisy has a face

You claim truths which are unreliable,
Facts that are no doubt fictional,
Embrace fabrications as if true,
Disregard details that exist as evidence,
Censor with the intention of falsifying history,
Since truth makes you a traitor, a martyr, a victim.

That is to say, you lie to exist.

Kafé Korais, Athens, 29 September 2007

You left leaving

I love thee
though you are gone
Now, free to wander.

I love thee
praise the restless seas, *a destiny's misfortune*
fleeing into my embrace
(Salty taste left on the mouth)

I love thee
poetry from a land you left
translate in each glance
(Stroking dry fingers on perfumed skin)

I love thee
a tone too dark to be greeted
I stand in the church without you
(Grasping a photograph and creased letter)

I love thee
youths dye rocks with your blood
head under steel toe boot, *tattoos identity*
(Waiting for that phone call)

Athens, 29 September 2007

Identity

I will become
What we all end up as in the end –

A Synonym.

Athens, 5 October 2007

Another day

A silk shirt wrinkles
on the living room floor,
next to a pile of *Athens News*.
It's that time after work
when the cat purrs.
NET News is about to start.
She unzips a tailored skirt,
soon to climb the stairs,
open the bedroom door;
but till then, her shadow
is examined through the curtain.

Athens, 24 January 2008

Meeting of the Holy Synod

The day he departed
with an early morning pause,

the mountains that bounded Athens
were silenced by incessant snowfall,
wayward rivers ran mercilessly
washing faith in all directions,
rolling clouds confiscated the light,
thunder pined through the gloomy skies,
twice striking the human ear.

Braving the cold,
emos, desperate for another Messiah,
rallied at the steps of the church
in black jeans, patched by anxious mothers,
debuting new faces stripped of piercings;
their shivering bodies and gritted teeth, ignored.

But believers understood,
that when the trumpets blew
to announce that a preacher had entered,
and the existing hour was brought to a halt,
that they were now without a shepherd.

Nea Penteli, Athens, 28 January 2008

REBIRTH

Flowers began to blossom in our tiny village,
the morning he arrived – that white dove.
Rejoicing in spirit, we laughed,
our hearts bursting with love.

Athens, 28 January 2008

IN HIS *M*EMORY

Amazed how *he* could have done it
Forgive them in that way

Was she supposed to take pity on
the baker who deprived her of change,
the boss for giving the job to his niece,
the husband who bedded her sister…

The beggar, pocketing twenty pounds,
prayed for pardon before nailing her to the wall,
arms pointed at the heavens

to know *his* pain

A man whose heart was far greater
than her own.

Athens, 5 February 2008

Playing god

for Nanos Valaoritis

A momentous occasion/ that blank screen/

you meet again like old friends/ face to face/ no ostracising/ no games/ just pure unabridged fiction/ you're loyal that way/ hoping the words will appear without your contribution/ for a story to unravel in front of your very eyes/ you welcome the thought/ consider the possibilities/ envision the adaptation/ thrilled at the prospect/ the chance to be spared/ liberated from the unbearable sweating and sleepless nights/ ideas cropping up during that morning beverage/ or when soaking in the bathtub trying to erase the day's troubles/

nose stuck in the newspaper/ hiding the cigarette that made you an outcast/ you think back to when your smudged notebook rested by a mug of coffee and that faithful packet/ why must it all change you sigh/ they were the times most favoured/ the days when you wrote epics/ wishing/ once more/ to exhale fiction with the same ease writers exaggerated in the back rooms of the pubs and cafes/

the silence disturbs you/ sickly nostalgic for the sound of your old typewriter/ a computer knows only how to whisper/ *tap-tap tap-tap*/ you believe that words are not earned when fingers do not ache/ surprisingly it pleases you/ no more arthritis or doctors' bills/ nevertheless/ you are saddened/ for the intimacy has vanished/ the words don't carry their weight/ before the infinite word counted/ before you thought of each one meticulously/ before the ink pressed them on paper/ key after key/ now there are many/ lines full of words/ effortlessly deleted/ copied/ cut and pasted/ you want your words to be felt/ a muted keyboard suggests secrets/ you write for it to be read out loud/ shouted over the Thames/ you have nothing to hide/ which is why you want your laptop to scream obscenities/ for the writing has to acquire movement/ so that the characters journey through the story/ you grow susceptible to their every whim/ you have not learnt to betray/ (not up to now)/ a victim of your characters' flaws/ you reinvent yourself within the body of the text/

a writer beckons for a breath/ struggling to separate their life from the imaginary other/ the reality doesn't seem so satisfying/ wondering who has stolen whose life/ you or your protagonist/ what does it matter/ you are indisputably alive/ breathing aspirations/ unfaithful to persons walking in and out of your study/ regretfully/ you don't budge/ you can't/ since what you have in front of you is a far greater gift/ the truest gift/ a soul's turbulent adventure/ your creation/ how exhilarating/ to be able to compose in a way that prevents others saying what they wish to but fear to/ you/ a master of letters/ leaves them vulnerable/ searching for themselves in the unbound manuscript/ afraid that their weaknesses have been recorded/ as you are a witness to their being/ though your fascination lies further than the familiar/ they are of no interest/ it is the woes of strangers that have caught your fancy/ faithfully following their shadows/ footsteps/ what their hands have touched/ you are driven by their discretion(s)/ vulnerabilities/ you compile motives for their actions/

weeks and months race by/ your final draft is ready to leave the room/ come up against the critics/ when it reaches other hands/ it is seen differently/ on occasions not appreciated/ underestimated/ opinionated men dictate what you can and can't say/ and how you should say it/ in other words/ the way in which to express yourself/ they question the experiments with narrative style/ the tendentious tone/ nationalistic sentiment/ your dogmatic approach/ they stand confident/ trends change/ you grin/ as you pass the private clubs where your name has been mentioned/ yet you obey/

You become a brand/ an enterprise/ named the next Beckett/ Joyce/ it all becomes impersonal/ what happened to the literary endeavour/ when did your pen start to imitate your contemporaries/ or scholars from public schools start meddling with the anarchists of the fictional page/ hadn't their predecessors judged unfairly in the past/ when masterpieces found themselves lost amongst a slush pile/ that was when small printing houses were more courageous/ when movements evolved/ schools of writers were established/ surely/ how can they know what they themselves have not executed/ so adamant to judge the unfamiliar/ read they say/ it's all in the reading/ you refer to them as parasites/ the outsiders/ the men who could never write that one accomplished novel/ gleaming with eagerness to tarnish the ones who dared/ and succeeded/ asserting power without hesitation or guilt/

regardless/ your salvation rests in the readers/ you wrote it for Them/ you/ the storyteller in search of an audience/ it needed to be said/ which is why/ impatiently/ you wait/ grateful for some feedback/ to confirm whether you had done right/ introduced some kind of justice/ for your main character/ for yourself/ so that when leaving your house every morning you'd feel assured that you chose well/ that you let your protagonist go without remorse/ freeing yourself from responsibility/ finally able to return to the life of a recluse/ ready to confront the new idea waiting for a beginning.

Athens, 12 February 2008

War

(her) bitten fingernails reap the scalp,
religiously peeling at raw skin. Blood
falls, like pellets into winter water.

as a day ages, its waste journeys down the river,
pleasing thirsty lips of a forgotten village,
not far from the olive tree where she stands.

Kolonaki, Athens, March 2008

LOVE

He settles for combing her long strands:
ninety-eight, ninety-nine, a hundred…

a lover's hand reaches for the bucket,
pouring water over her head

in one Noachian flood,
releases her.

Kolonaki, Athens, March 2008

FAITH

A baby's wailing charges through the aisles,
gurgling trickles of holy water between immersions,
supported by unfamiliar hands, paddles like a fish.
The priest's fumbling fingers seek the scissors,
snipping four locks of uncut hair, crosswise,
whilst the hundred bear witness.

Kolonaki, Athens, March 2008

Friends, Indeed!

I feel free, Madame Bloom: the Northern wind has cleansed me.

You kneel before sculpted flowers, eager to recreate a village
seen through skimmed postcards by a sender you wished to ignore.

I, on the other hand, forgot to water mine,
last year's Christmas present – shrivelled like prunes.
Funny, it was as if you'd expected it.
Yet you didn't utter a word. I've come to accept
that you've been silenced by a genocide you rarely mention.

To you, my lady, I am faithful, a fact you can't deny.
Pleasing you with my bourgeois ways and discreet departures.

Unexpected that Southern wind, knocked me to the ground.

An omen. I'm sure you'll agree.

Athens, 13 March 2008

in Giving

Give me love,

I will give you bread and water to calm a bellowing gut
that despairs over rumours of drought.

Give me books,

I will give you clothes to comfort weather-beaten bones
bruised by the cold bite that grinds humour dry.

Give me music and dance,

I will give you soap to scrub tired hands gashed by a barren soil
that once fed a village mocked for their jolly bellies.

Give me art,

I will give you local beauty, a muse excused from love,
bartered in a bar brawl to fill a father's empty pockets.

Give me a bed,

I will give you visions to nurture a starving imagination
wounded by the isolation of a land and its apocalypse.

Nea Penteli, Athens, 18 September 2008

THE 𝓑LINDING LIGHT CIRCLING ELPIDA, IN ONE ACT

[Evening. Central Athens.
Backstage at the theatre. Elpida's dressing room.
An hour before the curtain goes up, Alexandra approaches Elpida, concerned about her actions. Elpida appears distressed.]
Time – Present

Elpida, what are you doing?
You, as my witness, can surely answer that, my dear Alexandra.
This is what worries me, that my sight deceives me.
I am brushing my hair, you senile woman.
But my sweet girl, they shaved it off. Remember?
I know that. Do you think I am mad, or that I have forgotten?
Do you?
[She pauses.]
He has to have heard my prayers. Has he not?
What sort of a question is that? Of course, he has.
If only I could see him, hear his thoughts.
If only he would grant me the opportunity to discuss my options,
so that I can ask where I went wrong.
Wouldn't that be marvellous?
But I have faith, do you hear? Faith! Even though…
What alternative do I have? A beggar's choices are little or none.
Faith is all that remains.
It gives me the courage to get through each day with dignity.
So I have decided that I must go on as usual.
Nothing will change, do you hear?
Every morning, I will sit in front of that mirror and brush my hair:
a hundred strokes for a hundred prayers that this will all go away.
Yes, I have made up my mind.
I have decided that I am not going to waste
what little strength I have dwelling on a what if.
Hear! Hear!

[Alexandra dances around the dressing room
with a wine glass in her hand.
Several times, she loses her balance
when one foot clumsily treads on the other.
Meanwhile, Elpida drops her robe in front of the mirror.
The truth of evolution is evident in her reflection.
She puts on the theatrical costume, ready for her final performance.]
The last few nights on stage,
I saw my mother in the front row,
shedding tears of joy.
In her hand, she held the handkerchief I had bought;
it was a gift for her birthday.
She was my only audience,
and I the only performer on that stage.
She watched in admiration, listened intently.
Then she gave me an approving grin.
I remember that smile.
She had not stopped smiling that particular smile
since that memorable day:
the day the dictatorship collapsed.
She threw herself at my father and cried the same tears of joy,
saying again and again,
'We're free, Aristotle.
We're finally free from those barbarians.
Are you listening? We've been liberated!'
She grabbed my father's hand, lifting him to his feet,
twirled him around the room,
the same way you were twirling,
shouting at the top of her voice,
'We're free! We're free!'
I have played that scene repeatedly in my head
so that I would never forget her smile.
The year she fell ill, sadness overwhelmed her,
and that smile was lost.
But mankind will always be enslaved,
either by government, or by health.
We, as Greeks, have always been a condemned race.

But proud and brave – we must never ignore that fact.
This is why you must fight like a hero, as you have in the past.
Do you hear me?
I hear you, God. I hear you.
Elpida, it was me. It was me who was talking to you.
Who did you think it was? Who were you speaking to?
The miracle I was waiting for.
Life once more is answering my pleas.
A great soldier always dies a hero. Is that not what you once said?
But you're one of our country's national heroes,
my beautiful Elpida.
Courageous and important on both stages:
as a leading actress – and a woman.
[Elpida lifts her glass to propose a toast.]
Long live the freedom of companionship!
Long live the freedom to love!
And, long live the comforts of our motherland, my compatriot!
[They clink glasses.]
To our history!
To deliverance!
And let's not forget the most important. To good health!
[They raise their glasses once again.]
From your mouth to God's ear.

CURTAIN

[End]

Cinque Cafe, Newtown – Sydney, 18-19 May 2009

THE COLUMN

La Torre Pendente di Pisa failed to stand vertically.
Specialists blamed this on its poor foundation.
Her column followed a different school of thought;
a pillar whose strength rivalled that of the Pentelic marble,
yet suffered considerable damage from a playground mishap.

Unlike Frida, she picked up the pen,
employing a battalion of words,
imprints of a lost childhood, abundant phrases
feuding backbiting tongues and discourteous stares:
'A curse of the illiterate,' her mother swore.
For a while she walked on stilts, transforming flatties
to freaks in a touring sideshow;
crayons and felt tips coloured in kingdoms, distant lands
where she subdued the sanctimonious drivel of princesses,
secured the admiration of knights and kings, sentenced traitors,
consoled peasants, adhered to the teachings of ancient prophets –
here, her pagan eyes were compared to flawless emeralds.
Boredom helped create a world
where she was permitted to intervene,
but even this distraction could not protect her from the fisted hand
striving on paper to bow to the one reality,
that she, like the tower, might topple.
Frequent rendezvous with Hippocrates's disciples displeased her,
morning breaths unkindly met; meticulous sculptors
strapping her torso with bandages, fitting her for a bespoke corset –
the smell of drying plaster repeatedly made her gut churn.
So she shut her eyes, migrated to a self far from the common folk
where her beauty equalled Helen of Troy's and Lady Guinevere's,
reflecting on whether Waterhouse would have been as kind
as he was in his depiction of 'Circe Poisoning the Sea'.
'Beauty is only skin deep,' her father promised,
barely in school uniform
when the pointing of fingers persecuted her.

As a pupil, she walked hopeful,
having learnt that the skill of writing could make her notable.
Her scribbled notes spoke of society and the perils of women;
she refused to accept that the plight of Austen,
Woolf, Plath… went unrewarded.

Her column would be restored. Now a swan in a crowd,
she followed the gift inspired by a prolific imagination,
she crossed into the real world where she'd gaze
from the decks of ships, from port to port,
out of plane windows that carried her across
the unkempt and barren landscapes of foreign continents.
In these adopted hometowns, she would be compensated,
taken aback by the rewards bestowed upon the future:
an illustrious history of literary garlands,
accolades that firmly established her reputation
as a distinguished woman of letters.
'The pen in time forgives all,' she said at a news conference.
These words forced scholars into the donated archive
of a university library,
scavenging for truths, frustrated at their inability
to decode the wit that had eased her journey,
fictional oeuvre that served as a testimony to the stone years.

Bangor, Wales, 22 July 2010

Tree of misfortune

It was inevitable that the sentiment of love
would fade from the widow's eyes,
the harm inflicted upon her was irreparable
once sorrow put down roots,
and buried the loss in the core of the cortex,
allowing the deceased to resurface
at her beck and call.

Circumstance transformed a character
the locals spoke fondly of
into a woman whose grief had overtaken her,
and rightly so.
Daily, she fought to hold onto
the measly portions of affection that still persisted
to prevent her turning into a dying animal
feasting on the disappointments of others,
seeking pleasure from the wounded.
For this reason alone, she was understandably excused
when outbursts of uncontrollable resentment
poured out of this housewife collapsed in her chair,
perched like a statue where time, expression, and goodwill,
had been simultaneously frozen.
She despised all when her dearest Emmanuel was taken ill,
not long after he was made redundant from a job
he had remained committed to right to the last day.
'A shortage of doctors,' staff explained,
cautious about offering expressions of sympathy
to this grandmother who had anticipated retirement
with her loving husband.
She had planned to accompany him to Meganisi,
his childhood playground,
a secret peering through the hidden curtains of Lefkada:
the island where music metamorphosed into words
that balanced like thirsty leeches on poets' lips,

words that enticed skilful and willing hands to record
histories, tragedies, and prophetic visions.

London grew damper after his premature farewell;
it stopped the anguished wife
from speaking further neighbourly words.
How disheartening the economic crisis was to the romantic,
and to the optimist who imagined a different horizon,
with the passing of each falling star exhaling the sky.

Nea Penteli, Athens, 6 October 2010

Interrogating the Gunman

At a bus stop in Hampstead,
she turned her attention to the commuter beside her,
top to bottom in brown tweed,
sitting calmly in 5-degree weather.
He passed the minutes
watching bibliophiles walk in and out of Waterstones,
whilst readjusting a ground-grazing overcoat;
even after several failed attempts
he refused to abandon the task.
A moment's daydream triggered her memory of
Abbott's 1928 portrait of James Joyce;
like Joyce, he wore his fedora hat at an obvious slant,
except *his* walking stick was positioned across his knees.
He seemed a man of military bearing,
pale and drawn,
exhibiting signs of post-war fatigue.
It's coming in 19 minutes, the 46, he said,
as he struggled to tame an unruly moustache with his forefinger.
In 8, she replied, it's changed;
the red letters flickered on the announcement board
adding lurid colour to drab light.
Can you speak another language? he asked.
Greek, she answered.
I know a few words from a Greek-Cypriot friend, he said:
Χριστὸς ἀνέστη, καλημέρα, καλησπέρα, πούστης;
not a good word the last, he added
(the left side of his mouth held a half smile).
But used all too often, she assured him.

(She found it odd that his command of Modern Greek
included the phrase Χριστός ἀνέστη, 'Christ is risen',
a greeting traditionally exchanged during Easter.)
What other languages do you speak? she asked.
German, French, Latin, Ancient Greek, he replied.
It's here, she said,
relieved to see the bus turning into the High Street.
He got up with a groan, towering over her,
every small step met with a moan.
The bus kneeled for him to enter,
his every stagger more painful than the next.
In front, French students
continued their tête-à-tête undisturbed;
she offered her seat instead, but he declined,
he preferred to shuffle towards the seats nearest the rear door.
Three stops, he said,
miscalculating the distance to where he was to get off.
She stayed close in case he required assistance:
an indication of good breeding, many would agree.
Teşekkür ederim, he responded,
as he hobbled unsteadily off the bus at Kentish Town
with a moan, groan, and stagger.
He had left her speechless with the language
he chose to express his gratitude,
having struck her with his callous wit… in the foot.
Clearly, old age had made him bolder, and thus
permitted him to live out his spite with no major regret.

Bangor, Wales, 2 February 2011

Alitheia

The Greek truth –
is it not every man's truth,
that the written word of the poet
in its finality, will be,
as we will come to know it,
our only trusted ally?...

Bangor, Wales, 13 February 2015

PART 2

Athens, 1993

The Demon and the Hero

I.

Athens.

How they violated her.
Left her bare.
Intruded on her history to claim it as a part of theirs…
How soon they forgot that it was she who nourished life into their seed.
That it was her children who fought in her honour;
but when they raised their wings to strike,
the wind was fated to change direction.

Αθήνα.

Ορθοδοξία ....Orthodoxy
   Πάθος .... Passion
    Περηφάνεια .... Pride
      ΕΛΕΥΘΕΡΙΑ .... FREEDOM
Ζωή .... Life

Never, the Death…

Athens.

I remembered watching the tiredness in her eyes.
Listened to the stories of men who spoke of her spirit.
Men who died with her name engraved on their lips.

We shan't forget her cries in the middle of the night.
We shall never cease to witness her voice on the pages devoted to her…
or of the lovers destined to follow her.

I remembered this city.
Her struggles.

I remembered my uncle.
A proud man. Captain of the waters.

I remembered him well.

A victim of hers.

II.

I'll fall down the cliff. I'll fall. Hold onto me. He says from his hospital bed.
Now I go left, and right.
Be careful of the cot. How much money is over there?
Take it down from there, before the wood falls. He moves his hands up and down in the air to shift it.
I left my hand at the shop.
My two daughters are called Eva. Who's there?
I cannot turn.
Look at the odd hens, rabbits, snakes.
Inside my jacket. Eva, you'll fall.
He grabs at the air.

Nurse says: 'It's as though he has done terrible wrongs. Nothing he has seen is good, always strange… unpleasant.'
He is now blind. The morphine ceases to have an effect on him. He looks straight ahead. Round and round. His eyes are wide open.

Get up now, Gloria. I want to lie down. Come on Eva, get up from there.
I'm going down now. Am I going down quickly?
I'm unwell at the moment, later.
Who said it? Oh my! Oh my! It came out from there.
Katerina, where are you going?
That windowpane is broken. It needs repairing. He lifts his hand.
Hold this.

The nurse says she hasn't seen anything like this in twenty years as a nurse. The morphine is not working, and all he sees is traumatic. He is too scared to close his eyes.

The police are beating the thieves.
Don't beat them! Don't beat them!
Drag them away from there, Eva.

Let me go outside. Twenty-four. Press it so that it goes to thirty-four.

He lifts his tensed body. He attempts to hold onto whatever is within reach.

Be careful you're not thrown down.

Come over this side. He latches onto my arm and hauls me to the other side of the bed. *Come over here.*

How many metres is it from here? Are you calling out for Irini? Who's crying now? Irini is shouting. They're hitting Katerina. Oh jeez, Katerina is crying. Turn it back. Is it possible they're hitting the girl? The school is on the phone. Who's crying?

Hey! He screams out.
Who's driving the car? The dog, the white dog, will take the bag. Go get the bag. Go!
There, it's there. Where is it? Hey, where are you going?
Did it steal anything?
Take it down now. Why hasn't it started?
I can't bear it; I'm roasting.
He is drenched in sweat.
Put it on SKAI TV. Switch the light off in there.
Eva, change it. Good heavens, I don't want to see it. Turn it off. Turn off four, thirty-one, thirty-one.

Katerina! Hey, Katerina, do you happen to know whether I have to switch off the light… switch off the light? Did you switch it off?

Nurse says: 'What anxiety, folks. What is this?'

His hands moved, picking up imaginary objects, repositioning objects, lifting objects in mid-air.

Oh, friend! Close the door up there.
Move further back, friend.
Anna, pick up the sweater.
That one there on the floor.
I can't take it anymore, Eva. I'm about to burst.

I'm hurting from the pain. You don't know how much I'm suffering. What am I going to do?
My stomach is in pain.
What bad luck!

For goodness' sake! He raises his hand and grabs at something.

Take this my fine man, and hang it over there. Throw it there in the corner.

Which Vangelis?
What is he?

What is that? They operated on me.

Go, Katerina, Eva. Go.

He tries to pull out the drip with his teeth.

We are told that the hallucinations are brought on by a reaction of one drug with another.

Remove your head from there, Katerina.

He pulls things out of the bed and inspects his palm.

Move from there, Katerina. Move from there, my fine man.
My fine man, it's thirty-one. It's thirty-five, brave man.

Petros is coming on Sunday. They fixed the road. Was he here?

Sh!! Be quiet.

Eva, push me. I want you to hold me so I can make my way across. She's waiting for me. Eva is waiting for me. Take hold of me, will you.

We help.

Eva's just walked in.
It's ten drachmas, seriously.

Do you want the yellow? Is it the yellow that you want?

The car is going to pass by any minute now, and I'll go to sleep.
We'll turn. Let's go round and round to turn.

We'll fall and get badly hurt.
Mother of God!
Fearful, he glances around the room.
He'll kill us.

Nurse says: 'I will go home sick.'

Thank you for your kindness.
Come on, my friend, your mother's been unwell for two years! Sick!

What? Where is the girl?
He looks up in shock. *What?*
Anna, child!
Who's that? Why is Anna crying?

Go and get the medicine.
It's a good distance. Run. Run, Katerina.

Dear God, where am I going now? He stares at us with dread.

Why are we not going down? Who's talking now?
What? Have they got a problem with us?
He clutches at something.
Did they throw away the syringe?
He grasps an object on his stomach.
We ask him what it is. He says: *A syringe.*

Where is Katerina? She has still to come today.

He grabs at things in the air.

I will get down and go to sleep below.
It's the metal, so it doesn't press against my foot.
I don't know, daughter. I can't, guys.
Don't say the prices. What will he say, my child? We don't have the time to change it.
Let me be, Eva; I have been tormented for ten years.
Take the plates away, will you. Stop!

The night before, the second nurse said: 'Fifteen years and I have never experienced this before. With all the drugs he has taken, he is supposed to be sedated. He is talking and doesn't stop.' The third nurse said: 'He is like an addict now suffering from hallucinations.'

I'm sorry, young lady. I'm sorry, my fine man. I'm sorry, sir.

A thousand apologies. I am sick and…

What happened? Come!

Tell Eva 'okay'.
I hear her.
I will see her in the evening.

I bought your hand.
They have climbed high up in the mountain.
Spiros, pass me the telephone.

He starts to speak in English. *Athens! Greece! Hellas!* His wife, Gloria, gives him water. She asks whether he wants anymore, and he replies, returning to his native Greek: *The gentleman gave me water to drink.*

Hey, come here. Leave it, will you. Damn it!
Sorry! Sorry! He whistles loudly.
My God! Oh my!
Excuse me, my friend. We'll fall down; keep that in mind.
Christ and the Virgin Mary preserve us! He crosses himself.
Tell me, sir. He then says in English, *tell you, sir…*
Again, he reverts to his mother tongue.

There you are. We will come back.
I tell him that Katerina is having her birthday.
He says, *Fifteen.* I say, Sixteen. *I forgot,* he says, *that's right, they're closed on the twenty-fifth.*
We tell him not to move his hand.
He says: *It's like this because I'm sick.*
Thank you. Thank you very, very much.
May God be always with you.
Hello, my boy. Come! Come!
If you would be so kind as to sit down there, madam, so I can see if I threw the blanket.
I won't have a key. Come, my brave man, give me your hand. Three, three. What was that?
He is near to tears. *Call seven one. Tell them we have fallen from the line. Call Petros. At the Italian's, at the Englishman's, for Petros's house. At Sotiropoulos's. Call seven one.*

Stand up to them, Eva.
Forbid them, Eva.

Hold me up a little so that I can arrange the papers.

Eva, consult with Irini.
Yes, my child. Tell him 'okay'. Put it inside. Why does it work like that?
I'm not in the mood, Eva. I am in a great deal of pain and meanwhile I can barely stand.
I'm not able to speak, Eva.
Today, we really got into a fix.
Get it out, Spiros. The paper.
Spiros, Spiros. Take that one out, will you.
Take it, Spiros. The papers here, Spiros.

III.

Imprisoned by illness, his struggle had at times denied him the will to live.

Those who were in his presence, particularly the doctors and nurses, said that it was a miracle that he was still alive. The reasons, we quickly understood, were transparent. On a Saturday evening, he was to witness in his hospital room the engagement of his eldest daughter. He held on until then. 'I'm leaving, I know,' he said. And he would weep that he would not be there to marry her off. What's more, his brother, Petros, would be coming from Australia. So he would hold on until they were reunited. The doctors had predicted that he would not live to see his brother set foot on Greek soil. How wrong they were.

More than a week had passed since the arrival of his brother when we were informed that he would die that night. His eldest daughter, Eva, nineteen at the time, had planned to sleep in his room. I accompanied her.

'Don't be afraid, you're not alone. I'm here beside you,' his daughter said to him.

'You have to let him die. You're making him suffer.
He won't die, because you won't let him,' the nurse told me.
She turned to his daughter. 'It's time,' she said.

The nurse requested that she refrain from touching him to allow him to die and his soul to rest.

The nurse asked him whether he wanted something to eat. No, he answered. His daughter let go of his hand, and I held onto hers. His breathing got slower and less frequent. His tears could not be contained. He let out a loud yell. Angry. He wanted to live... to fight... and he could not. He would take three more breaths... determinedly. He yelled for the second time, but this time it was as if he was at peace and wanted to rest. It was more a sigh – an intense sigh – indicative that his soul had parted from his body. He took one last breath, and with that, he had departed one life to enter another. Then, not long after, the hospital workers undressed him and commenced the washing of the body with wine.

In an act of absolution, I went back into the past... to the failings of the pathologist (the family doctor), and his inability to question the root of one man's illness... to the professor of surgery whose effort to treat the sick depended on the extent to which he was able to line his own pocket... The truth was bitter.

Death was no ally, not in war nor in illness.

IV.

Athens, blossoming deception.
Disease starves your womb.
Naive are those eyes. Blinded is your soul.
Filthy is the blood that shrieks in your hands.

Now we perish, sweet mother Athens.
For you kill the kind.

Biography

Born in Sydney to Greek parents, Dina Kafiris earned her undergraduate degree at the University of Western Sydney, during which she studied Ethics (Philosophy) at Deree – The American College of Greece. She subsequently moved to the UK. Her poetry, fiction and essays have appeared in *Mōnolith: Visuals & Verses, Wild Court, American, British and Canadian Studies, The Journal, Nea Synteleia, Horizon Review* and *Odyssey Magazine*, among others. She was a regular member of and collaborator with the Corais group of the Greek literary review *Nea Synteleia* (New End of the World), under the Greek poet Nanos Valaoritis. Her poetry chapbook, *The Blinding Light Circling Elpida, in one act*, was published by Original Plus in 2014 and is from her forthcoming trilogy *21st-century Modern Greece: The First Decade*. She holds an MA in Creative Writing from the University of Leeds and a PhD in Critical and Creative Writing from the University of Wales, Bangor. She was Writer in Residence and Guest Lecturer at Kingston University London.

Kafiris is a Fellow of the Royal Society of Arts.

About KU Press

Kingston University Press has been publishing high-quality commercial and academic titles for over ten years. Our list has always reflected the diverse nature of the student and academic bodies at the university in ways that are designed to impact on debate, to hear new voices, to generate mutual understanding and to complement the values to which the university is committed.

Increasingly the books we publish are produced by students on the Kingston School of Art MA courses, often working with partner organisations to bring projects to life. While keeping true to our original mission, and maintaining our wide-ranging backlist titles, our most recent publishing focuses on bringing to the fore voices that reflect and appeal to our community at the university as well as the wider reading community of readers and writers in the UK and beyond.

@KU_press

This book was edited, designed, typeset and produced by students on the Kingston School of Art MA Publishing course at Kingston University, London.

To find out more about our hands-on, professionally focused and flexible MA and BA programmes please visit:

www.kingston.ac.uk
www.kingstonpublishing.wordpress.com
@kingstonjourno

Milton Keynes UK
Ingram Content Group UK Ltd.
UKHW010819220424
441551UK00004B/340